Contemplative Listening

ROBERT SARDELLO

Goldenstone Press Granbury, Texas

Published by

Godenstone Press

417 Doyle

Granbury, Tx 76084

About The Author

Robert Sardello, Ph.D. work concerns integral spirituality – the dynamic, creating, unity of body, soul, spirit, Earth, and the Divine. This work began in 1992 with the founding of the School of Spiritual Psychology with Cheryl Sander- Sardello. He is the author of eight books including *Silence: The Mystery of Wholeness, Heartfulness, Love and the Soul: Creating a Future for Earth, Freeing the Soul from Fear, And The Power of Soul: Living the Twelve Virtues*. The most recent unfolding of integral spirituality includes seminars concerning awakening to the Spiritual Earth, and the Wisdom of Eldering.

Also By Robert Sardello

Facing the World with Soul

The Power of Soul: Living the Twelve Virtues

Freeing the Soul from Fear

Love and the Soul: Creating a Future for Earth

Steps on the Stone Path

Monographs

The Art of Cultivating Spiritual Imagination

Money as Spiritual Practice

Care of the Senses

Guide to Experiencing Destiny

A Soul Way of Forgiveness

Soul Activism

A Fairy Tale for Spiritual Psychology

The Gospel of St. John as a Foundation of Spiritual Psychology

Contemplative Listening

Table of Contents

I. Introduction

The purpose of this monograph is to increase our capacities of receptivity, under the general term of *listening* (although more than just hearing is implied). Listening here refers to attending to others and the Earth in new ways, and it also refers to a more pervasive way of being-in-the-world. During several decades of research in spiritual psychology, I have developed ways to deepen a capacity of *inner waiting* to hear--within the heart and soul--what is expressed at the soul and spirit level by a speaker, or by the world, and—significantly—by Earth herself.

When listening matters, matter listens, going beyond what occurs only among people to enter what I call the Listening Cosmos of Wisdom.

We live within a pronouncement civilization. In Western culture today, too little is written or spoken concerning receptivity and even less about meeting others, world, and Earth in such a way that we experience being united with what is around us. We remain separate by defaulting to what our desires dictate. When merely mutual assertion rules our relationships, we *say* without simultaneous listening and hear only information.

It is not possible to know where we belong within a wholly pronouncement-oriented universe. Such a cosmology, the current cosmological metaphor of the Big Bang, can only expand. We live—sometimes unconsciously but always decisively—within a *pronouncement model* of the universe. An expansion cosmology reveals itself in daily life as an over-confident intellectuality, exaggerated emotional reactions, and an imposition of will. Within this kind of culture, opinions lob back and forth between people, one person pouring forth pronouncements, intellect, and views while the other person waits for a turn—not to respond, but to do the same thing back to the other person. If we can learn to wait politely or to mirror back to others what they just said, then we imagine we have learned some real techniques of listening, but have not entered listening.

This writing intends to go much deeper than learning techniques. It speaks from within a *listening cosmos*, a cosmos of Wisdom. There could be a physics of continual creation, a continually creative process of rhythmic giving-receiving-re-giving, a physics with listening at its center.

Through attuning to Wisdom, we can come to be able to sense that we, others, and Earth exist in a deeper state of listening. Receptivity forms the most foundational creative act. If we can come to be listeners just as the Spiritual Earth is the receptive, listening heart of the universe, then daily living reorients, coming into harmony with the ways of the primordial unity of Cosmos and Earth.

The Crumbling of the Pronouncement Universe: its degradation into the Lie.

The Anonymous "They"

Before describing the process of Listening, it is important to develop awareness of the pronouncement universe and its destructiveness.

Pronouncement is the way collective consciousness shapes the organizing forms of civilization. All institutions—political, religious, scientific, educational, economic, ecological—are affected equally. Anyone still free of soul suffocation wrought by non-listening feels trapped into a narrow range of responding.

The pronouncement mentality makes a pseudo-world by implicitly fostering the anonymous "they" of groups: the politicians, corporations, churches, educators, lawyers, doctors, technologists. Even intimacies become abstract without knowing what happened. It is impossible to stand against the "they" without becoming another "they." Isolated ego-beings, the largest of all pronouncement groups, form the pronouncement group of the "me-me." Yet, caught in reaction, "me-centeredness" is are unable to open to the simultaneity of individual/oneness of spirit dimensions.

The inability to listen characterizes a strange quality of exaggerated bravado. Don't let the bravado of pronouncement fool you into thinking that this form of speaking and non-listening brings genuine confidence. Rather, it signals an escape from our most human condition of living in the “not-knowing” and thus from creative Wisdom. Surrender, not giving up or giving in but yielding to pervasive Wisdom, reveals being human.

To orient receptively requires living constantly within the questions, “Why am I here?" and "What is the here?” The answer unfolds as a lived answer: to surrender to Divine fullness within the living expression of Divine fullness, Earth. That is Spiritual Earth. Without this receptivity in whatever situation we enter, we seek the comfort of sameness guaranteed by the pronouncement universe.

The incapacity of true listening manifests as mentally disguised curiosity, the love of idle chatter about others, and the many distractions from living within the question, “Who am I?”

It is not difficult to locate how the failure of receptivity has invaded individual life, making soul presence with others and presence to embracing spirit presences impossible.

When the beings who inspire no-listening take hold of a nation, the end announces itself.

The fact you are reading this work, deeply interested in the concerns mentioned, indicates an engagement in spiritual practice that is very demanding. You are perhaps somewhere within the following phases of what we stumble through in coming to understand that to listen, not merely to follow the pronouncements of someone, requires an inner effort of great strength over a long period of time. The phases:

1. I feel general dissatisfaction with the roles the present world imposes upon us.

2. I then begin to visualize general abstract possibilities leading away from that fated way of life and become restless.

3. This restlessness can remain abstract and then begins to drop away as I enter into being among the anonymous, even to myself, unaware that self-anonymity has replaced self-presence.

4. If the tension of dissatisfaction can be sustained, the possibility of a new opening becomes clear and more individually meaningful.

5. Tension develops between the old way of life and the new but unknown, resulting in anxiety.

6. If this tension sustains, specific action gradually becomes clearer. Rather than continue living as complaint, the capacity of wanting to listen and to hear what may be both "above" and "beneath" the distractions of pronouncement arises.
7. If the awakening interest in opening heart and soul continues through the tension and anxiety, the isolated individual comes to experience embodied spirit presence, an open, receptive individuality, capable of full participation with others, and more significantly, with Earth.

However, there is an inner region that involves a leap. The phases described are not a natural evolution, where, at some point, you will feel the sense of fullness and inwardly know what it is like to be a listening being rather than someone who listens now and then. When you face this leap, it is not leaping to the other side, as it is leaping *into* a void rather than leaping *over*. Fear presences surround this void. It is possible to make such a leap only from the place of the interior of the heart as its very center is incapable of fear. The transformation into listening is a transformation into heartfulness.

II. The Silence of Heartfulness

True listening cannot come about from what someone else says to us unless said out of the Silence that also permeates us. Silence is required for true speaking and listening, and if what is said has no inherent Silence, we cannot listen. We can take in what is said and utilize it, as we do with information, for information has no Silence. But we cannot hear soul/spirit with uncreative utility.

The greatest vessel of Silence, always available, is the Natural World – Earth and all Her creatures. I do not mean that the Natural World lacks the capacity of language and is therefore silent. The Natural World speaks, but in such a manner that for Her, Silence is always in the foreground, felt as inspiration, awe, life, full breathing, heart-awakening.

As I listen to the rustling of the leaves of the trees outside my door, the rhythm of the breeze, the soft sounds, the delicate movement of the branches, pulls me into the Silence. It takes little attention to listen. All around us, a very different kind of cosmology from the one we have come to adhere to demonstrates itself. It is not at all that the Natural World speaks to us, we listen, and then respond, if only with a sigh of joy. To think of listening this way puts us back in the "pronouncement" universe. We have not really listened. Earth and the Natural World do not make pronouncements but rather make stunning expressions of invitation. We typically use the Silence of the world and Earth when She speaks, and the most we take in and feel is a moment of refreshment. There is so much more to listening to the Natural World.

We can be present with the Natural World in a primordial act of listening because the Natural World herself is a world of Listening! To say it directly and radically, *the world of Matter is the world of listening!*

The Greek word "physis,: from which we receive "physics"and "physical" originally means "a-rising," a "borning," emerging from the hidden—emerging every moment from the Silence, from the Stillness, which is Silence beyond the Silence.

The arising of things from the Stillness occurs as a whole, a unity. It is Wholeness coming-into-being without end. Thus, entering into the Stillness awakens us as a dimension of the active presence of Wholeness. Stillness is not divided up into parts, and it is itself not a part of anything; it is Wholeness itself. The ultra-silence of Stillness does not consist of the absence of noise, and it is more than quiet. The Stillness is a 'place beyond place within place,' all around us, within, beyond, below—everywhere, the 'land of no-where.' It's like that no-space space from which true art emerges, the so-called "negative space," where "negative" designates the non-materialistic, foundational, unending place of form originating, matter coming into being.

Here, with a fuller and truer meaning of matter, we enter into living within the cosmology of "giving" and "receiving" all that exists, where speaking matters. The word is the Word, the unity between the mythical and the literal. Deep truth, the true, cannot be known by intellect. The truth of reality opens with listening, so we must listen to enter contemplative understanding. Understanding occurs when the embrace of listening meets the embracing soul. There is nothing intellectual about deep understanding, for it is not a form of "knowing about" something, but of knowing within it.

Our usual modes of consciousness only hear bits and pieces, not recognizing the presence of the Whole. We presently engage awareness as if it were arrow-like, shooting out, bringing back only this and that, forming an incomplete view of reality "out there." Consciousness as a vessel has its precision, but it is not a vessel capturing parts for examination by the mind. The process of listening between people is only a rhythmic instance of symphonic reality sounding, a vibratory example of Cosmic-Earth Wholeness undivided.

When we listen, truly listen to someone, we abide within our place as Earthly spirit-beings, and we do something unusual. We do not hear words, but rather, *through* the words we hear the particularity of the Silence /Stillness as it configures itself into the moment. In order to listen, which has nothing whatsoever to do with the quiet we are in while someone is speaking, something else has to go on—hearing only the content has to be sacrificed every moment, given away, in order to hear the configuring of the Silence addressing us through what is speaking. The content becomes secondary to any particular moment of the Silence/Stillness reconfiguring into the Word that issues into the word.

Take a walk. Begin to listen to the Natural World you are within, and indeed, you are an aspect of the Wholeness, not just an observer capable of enjoying it all. Attempt to listen to the deep Silence/Stillness, mythic in dimension, of the physical world—not the given physical world typically noticed as if in front and around you. Beyond personal presence and prior to it, the body too belongs to Nature, and if we cannot listen through the body, we are not here. Such listening, while sensory, is vibratory, bodily, rather than taking place through the senses only.

Notice that the Silence is quite different as you stand and simply gaze at a tree, which itself has reorganized the Whole into its instance. Then go to a boulder and do the same thing, or to a plant, or anything else of the Natural World. Even each particular thing—one tree and next to it another tree of the same kind—speak the Silence very individually while within the fullness. Within the Silence, each presence gestures the Whole. The things of the Natural World do not speak language, so we are not interested in trying to put what they say within Silence into our language. Instead, feel the ongoing gestural-speaking presence of the physical world within the heart; hearing becomes rhythmic vibration.

III. Contemplative Listening with Others

Listening to another person does not suddenly leave the Natural World or Earth. But within receptive cosmology, conversing presents itself as a particular gesture of the Wholeness. Listening with another person can be a primary template for attuning to ever-present Wholeness-in-particularity.

To listen to another human being seems more challenging than to listen within the Natural World. Words seem to interfere, which is not the fault of words but of how we are with them. When we are with words as information, it is not possible to listen contemplatively. Informational hearing has become the primary way of paying attention to someone and focuses primarily on "getting it," that is, getting what the other person says. Having got it, a response is then lobbed back, not to show that we really "get it" but to "re-wrap" what we got within our interests while acting as if interested in the other person.

In contemplative listening, we hear something of the spirit-longing of the speaker; we hear a quest within the Silence, regardless of the content of the speaking, just as when we listen to the world around us—both the Natural World and the constructed world, we also begin to be present to their longings. What does a tree want? What does a building want? The answer is found by noticing the gestures present. The tree wants to be rooted, reaching for the sky. A building wants to hold and allow the inhabitants to experience soul; otherwise, it is not a true building but only an enclosure. The quest within the Silence gently holds living questions having to do with spirit-life that are more than personal or psychological matters. They are pre-personal, interpersonal, and transpersonal questions that address both the speaker and the listener. True questing hides within ordinary conversations. Questing hides, not out of fear, but to attract true listeners who are ready to listen.

People seek others to listen to them because they sense there is a felt quest they have not yet found. The word "question" opens itself when we hear the quest happening, and quest, not in pursuit of something, but as the ever arriving moment of the unknown disguising itself as-if known. The inner attitude of listening with another person then becomes one of embracing, together, the fullness, the pregnancy of the unknown.

When we are nagged or oppressed by a felt question, we do not feel ourselves, we are not inwardly at rest. And, when we converse with another from the place of questing, we are thrown out of the Stillness of our self into worldly motion.

The aim of contemplative listening does not consist of leaving the spirit-self but rather letting radiance to lovingly encompass the other person in what is being said. Self is not an abstraction but the embodied individual spirit that sees through the tricks of its shadow, the ego.

"How are you today?" We feel the question as being apart from spirit, as if we 'owned' our spirit, and from time to time risk reaching out from it, but not really letting go of the shadow of spirit, ego, for a moment. We are usually present only to our psychological reaction to the unknown questing living both within us and within others and remain unconscious that life quests.

A central concern of contemplative listening consists of developing the capacity to listen to and with felt questing of spirit. These questings within speaking and listening are experienced wordlessly within the word. Even the simplest speaking wordlessly concerns the deepest questions of existence such as death, freedom, meaning, values, soul, heart, relationship, and the Divine. Philosophy and religion approach such issues through intellectual engagement. Everyday conversation lives within them. The core of these themes is wordless, not questions that we have but questions that have us. Entering receptive consciousness requires surrender.

How to go about surrendering looms as a great concern regarding spirit. We cannot directly surrender by trying to do so because such attempts come from the place of ego, which never abandons its kingdom. Ego cannot be directly asked not to be ego. Although sometimes we do feel and come to the point of saying, "I give up," this constitutes surrender in a very narrow sense, an ego tactic of temporary retreat. Ego cannot be utilized to persuade itself into submission, which goes against its essential truth.

Still, ego has to be involved in the act of surrender. Those who have a spiritual practice, may, over many years, have come to temporarily recognize that surrendering ego has occurred due to the temporary shine of realities beyond ego. Indeed, there must be some genuine, authentic, and felt intuition of the presences of spirit realities, beings, worlds as right here, not "out there" in some other place. Such a realization can be a starting point for indirectly surrendering through a mantra that speaks to spirit realities as present, always. A mantra—a repeated word, sound, or sentence that continues to alter inner reality and outer perception—makes an opening of experiencing spherically and imaginally rather than linearly and literally.

Think of a sphere, think of it dimensionally, with something going on in one place of the sphere, say ego activity, while at another place of that sphere something of different qualities can be happening, like the intuiting of spirit presence. Ego, by itself, acts literally and linearly, moving from a linear sense of past into the present and anticipates a literal future, which is why, by itself, there is no way out of ego. A mantra, which is not particularly offensive to the inherently ignorant ego, speaks from another region of the sphere altogether and can open much larger, broader, deeper, higher dimensions than ego without bringing ego defenses to halt such a threat to itself.

Here is such a mantra – to be said gesturally, that is, not merely mentally, but felt bodily by gesturing the words with the lips, saying them aloud, and after a while, the phrase can be inwardly repeated over and over and over, silently: "I surrender to Divine fullness." This mantra can be said in times of contemplation, but it can and needs to be inwardly repeated throughout the day. Then the mantra sinks deeply into every dimension of the body, to the level of the cells. The mantra relaxes and enlivens the whole body. While previously the segmented-feeling body was filled with contradictory desires, it now reveals itself as the expression of our true self as an expression of the Divine. The repeated mantra suddenly becomes luminous, illuminates the body as spirit, defying the constructed notion of spirit as other than body.

Once this mantra can be bodily felt, somewhat like a bodily embrace from within, then start working to develop a specific, individualized mantra rather than this given one. Creating a mantra becomes a necessary step, for it will be a mantra suited to one's individual destiny. Develop the mantra by speaking different ones that are not thought up but that begins to emerge as a result of working with the given mantra. The arrival of a particular individual destiny-mantra will be unmistakably felt. It is unnecessary to know one's destiny and try to shape a mantra to suit. Rather, the intuited mantra shapes and encourages the seed of destiny we are here to complete.

Such a mantra becomes a lifetime mantra rather than a practice to be done for a while, a mantra of Listening awareness.

Who bears the spirit-question, the longing to experience the unknown future always arriving, prompting ongoing listening? When we inwardly hear a spirit-quest of someone within an ordinary conversation, it also becomes our question, arising as spirit confusion (con-fusion: "with fusion"). Such moments of confusion differ from unhealthy fusing with another. Only from the place of the heart can joining with another person at this level occur without the loss of individuality of both speaker/listener and listener/speaker. This kind of meeting with another constitutes the essence of contemplative listening.

With any spirit-talk, knowing and understanding effects change, but for the most part temporarily and at a surface level. Spirit acts; it is pure activity. Becoming more bodily, sensory spirit deepens and extends momentary change into the fabric and meaning of life. When, in usual forms of contemplation or meditation, where the practices require lessening body-presence to increase spirit-experience, the changes wrought by spirit presence do not last. The body remains dense and cannot hold the spirit action long. Becoming more *bodily* spirit-sensitive deepens and extends change and presence. The body itself has to undergo change, down to its physiology; this is the purpose of the mantra.

After a mantra is spoken for a period of time, bodily change is felt as a cascading of subtle, tremulous sensations spreading throughout the body when the mantra is silently spoken. These sensations are accompanied by changes of sensing the surroundings too. For a moment, the surroundings become embraced by invisible but palpable currents holding all particularities as a unity. The unity is always present. These first moments of experiencing the mantra's action merely make what is present become vividly present. Such moments feel magical or miraculous. The miracle has to be released in order to stay within what is happening and for such moments not to be captured and by that capture, deadened.

The result of staying with the mantra in this manner is the beginning of life becoming a contemplative life, a life of listening in the midst of usual, active, daily living. Every moment of listening becomes a spontaneous spiritual practice. Such moments do not accumulate fixed forms of knowing. Contemplative living continually creates un-knowing.

IV. Listening through Wholeness of Body-Soul-Spirit: The Body in Listening

When someone speaks, and we listen, not just with our ears, but centering in the heart, the speaking can be bodily felt in the listening, like an inner inaudible hum or perhaps like the resonance of harp strings. Trying too hard to understand the meaning of what someone says quickly covers bodily listening and conversing becomes either abstract or, sometimes, emotionally toned.

What spirit-soul-body registers does not first occur as if in the brain; the body receives spoken fullness rather than known words. To listen bodily is to be fully present, to fully feel the hum of the vibratory resonance of the waves arriving. Inwardly hearing in this way, warding off instantaneous but false knowing, is central in contemplative listening.

Bodily-listening centered in the heart registers as subtle bodily resonance. This resonance is its own way of knowing-as-being, something essentially wordless and thus pre-cognitive. Gradually, this resonance enters into harmony with the content heard and perceiving the person speaking changes for the listener. The person who is speaking glows. It is like listening to someone speak when there is a strong presence of love. However, with this kind of listening, the reactive, emotional component of love is not present, just pure love.

With contemplative listening, immediate intellectual understanding is sacrificed to stay present in the body with the resonance of the speaking. The body resonance occurring in listening bears a similarity to experiencing the body gesturing though the gestures are outwardly imperceptible. But they can be felt.

Contemplative listening can also occur in conversing with Nature.

I am sitting on the porch watching the trees—well, that is all the mind registers—and perhaps an emotional response of relief from anxiousness for a moment or a sigh of letting go. While such mental registration can be strong, it quickly dims. Attention shifting to the heart senses the world and simultaneously feels the body resonance. It awakens as symphonic presence rather than staccato concepts:

The rhythmic swaying of a tall tree in the background while those closer act like guardian sentinels of playful rhythms going on behind them. The sunlight touches a portion of the trees as the shadows reach back and engulf the leaves behind, darkening them into mystery. Through the thickness of the swaying and the quiet greening, the soft, light blue above shows through, revealing a different reality, a farness that is invited into the play of the rhythm, and indeed, feels as if it is the very source of the swaying green movement.

Listening-presence with others and with the world in this way lingers on after the experience. The nature of this lingering is important, for the lingering—felt bodily—softly tingles and is not just the memory of registering something that happened but rather a process in which the body itself undergoes cellular alteration. Such change of our own physical nature, in turn, alters the other person and also alters Earth. Such change is felt in the heart.

V. Deep Body-Listening

In listening while remaining completely open, not waiting to give an opinion or an emotion-based response, an awareness of the inner body occurs as guardian of the sacredness of receptivity. Again, this reception feels like the vibrations of a subtle inner-body humming or strumming. The body here is not the body of physiology, blood, organs, senses and skin, though it is the site of the vibrations. What is this inner sounding?

On the one hand, it is as if a person who just spoke transfers into the inner body of the listener and inhabits our soul without danger of harmful encroachment and resonates through the body, creatively changing us. We respond to the one who has spoken in ways that re-create the speaker, too—whether the speaker is a person, Nature, or the Earth.

The process has to be observed over a long period of time to notice such subtlety, but to take on such a practice is well worth the effort, for it leads to witnessing the miracle of ongoing creation. Human beings in true listening keep the world living!

Exhaustion results if deep body listening narrows to the region of the head only, or if one goes out of body while listening languishes and the listener leaves the actual for abstraction or fantasy. Non-listening not only drains one; it deals death. In a short time, the non-listener becomes like a completely predictable machine.

The way to avoid civilizational decay, which expresses listening decay, is to stay in-body and yet fully open. Being fully open while fully, sensorially present forms an alchemical kind of action within the vessel of the body, as well as between people and the Earth. Golden moments arise out of seemingly trivial talk.

Staying in-body does not mean concentrating on being present in the body for that is mental and thus doing the opposite of what is needed. Staying in-body means noticing currents bodily occurring when listening, which increase gentle concentration and interest while hearing the content alongside the rhythmic currents. That balancing has to be practiced.

Conversing enters into the vibratory force of another through the vibratory field of one's own body. It is like being in a musical field, hearing the content of the music while at the same time remaining completely bodily immersed in it and one with it. And, while within this I-Thou field, releasing trying to grasp everything heard melts away. When this kind of con-versing occurs, listening occurs as a form of mutual embodiment, as if within a ritual. Ritual-conversing, as *all* ritual, is always embodied; it is the embodied way of being connected as two-in-one, not just with another, but through mutual spirit/soul/body presence, joining with the wider encompassing worlds while remaining fully body-in-creation.

Ritual-like embodying with another also occurs as an act of complete identification with what the other person is saying. Any aspect of consciousness that remains as an onlooker or "on-hearer" temporarily disappears.

One further aspect of this phenomenological description of contemplative listening concerns presence with our whole being—body, soul, and spirit, with mind also present in in the background. When mind is not lovingly held by body, soul, and spirit, it starts to do business on its own, the forerunner and true meaning of artificial intelligence.

Listening with the mind only, abstract listening, even if it contains strong emotional content—as occurs in the pronouncement world, particularly in politics and in all collective consciousness—makes the listener subject to the qualities of the vibratory speaking of the other person, which enter as hypnotic suggestion. Nothing happens between people. They are enfolded into the pronouncements.

When I speak of remaining in-body, the term "body" here means the fullness of being human and at one with Earth.

It is not physical-only bodies or brains that see and hear, think and feel, walk and talk, breathe and metabolize, that speak and listen but embodied human beings. However, when human embodiment is abandoned while being with another, or with Earth, all of creation is simultaneously abandoned.

By body, I do not mean the physical body in our usual understanding of the body, but in the extended sense that was introduced earlier—*physis* as a-arising. The human organism. The word "organism" derives from the Greek verb *organizein*, to play on a musical instrument. The human organism as musical instrument resounds inner feeling tones, embodies them in muscle and nerve tone, cell and organ oscillation, the tone of voice, and the resonances of words and deeds. The organism is also the fullness of human bodily activity resonating directly with other human beings in listening. It was Aristotle who first spoke of the human organism as a purposeful and communicative instrument or organon of the soul. The soul is a skilled organist, which forms its organs while playing them.

VI. Wordless Listening: Giving Birth to Speaking

Listening is something more than a time interval taking place as someone speaks while we wait for the chance to speak in turn. This kind of technical listening can be detected when the mechanism adjusts. We find ourselves jumping in to speak before the other person has finished their thought and sentence. Only the outer human being is heard. Listening concerns the inner human being. The only access we have to the inner human being is through listening. But hearing the content of what someone says, even very attentively, is not listening. Listening is a wordless attunement that patiently and meditatively 'gathers' the felt inner sense, resonance, and essence of the speaker within what has been said.

Listening, as following the questing spirit-speaking of the other person, creatively builds toward a response. An inner after-image of the full spirit sense of what one hears builds. A tension gathers, and the art of conversing concerns allowing inner tension to build to exactly the right moment, so that responding occurs as an aspect of the rhythm rather than breaking into it. Such right-waiting often fails, resulting in feeling afterward that one was too hasty in wanting to join in the conversation. When it goes right, artistically, both speaker and listener enter new ways of being rather than going along pre-established tracks.

Contemplative conversation is an active form of wordless inner communication through which we can be present to the a-rising of our new self in conjunction with the other person undergoing similar new creation. Both people bear this new sense of self, but while it has not yet been birthed, a certain discomfort prevails if the birthing is in the pushing phase. The new can come forth when the discomfort is joyously held. Both individuals may feel uneasy, an uncomfortable excitement of something about to happen presents itself, and breaking it is to be avoided.

The emerging new selves have to be called-out through the listening process, a kind of midwifery. Thinking we understand interferes with the listening. A person instinctively knows when listening is not led by the inner voice of true being but merely hears along already heard and known tracks.

We begin truly to listen when we sense something lacking or questionable in our understanding. To maintain our listening means maintaining this continuous sense of not-understanding and relinquishing the urge to understand. To try and make the other person clarify what I do not understand as listener shuts listening down.

Access without harm to the inner being of another person occurs through the not understood. To make someone clarify the not-understood, so I can understand it means that I am making the person speak according to what I already know, also shutting down the emerging new self.

Maintaining listening to the not-understood is to be aware of a center of absolute Silence within ourselves where we hear nothing—that is, arriving at the center point of hearing. We have to become able to be present to this absolute inner Silence, even while listening. We learn to hold someone in our "aural gaze," similar to gazing into the eyes of a beloved. We know when we are listening when there is the felt quality of loving resounding through the words the other person speaks.

VII. The Gift of Contemplative Listening

Listening gives someone attention. That is a remarkable gift, the gift of spirit-being. Giving someone attention is an act, a doing that is something different than paying attention to what the other person is saying. Paying attention to what someone says feels like buying it. Someone speaks and you pay a little attention, retaining the rest of it as if valuable commodity. True attention is not like that, so paying attention does not utilize attention at all but simply restrains ego for a while, waiting to release it once again. Attention is whole and is either given or not.

Giving attention in listening is the act of holding someone in your attention. The one speaking feels held. That is the first moment of the gift of attention. What does being held in someone's attention feel like? Attention is not our intellect, nor our understanding, nor is it our feeling. Holding someone in our attention does not mean being sympathetic.

The great mystery of attention. We are our attention. Attention is not a couple of quarters we have in the pocket. Giving attention to someone gives our-self completely, nothing held back, complete vulnerability, something that can never be a matter of mere technique. Attention is the Silence itself. Giving attention gives inexhaustible Silence.

The capacity for listening is a spiritual path. It is not a technique that we can learn and then feel, "I've got it." It is a particular way of the unfolding of the individual spirit in the world, the way of becoming world, becoming Earth.

VIII. Responding: The Turning Point of Listening

Maintaining listening happens as a continuous sense of not needing to understand while being fully present; being within quietness of mind, vital, and emotional being, and adjusting to the bodily currents of whom we are with. Being within such empty-fullness, within body, feeling the field, invites the speaker into speaking from within the unknown. Receptivity invites receptive speaking, like the gentle pouring of water from an earthen vessel.

Receptivity is not passivity; it is a vessel-force that can be felt by the one speaking as welcoming, drawing what is unknown by the speaker into speaking from the place of open and alert emptiness. Listening gently takes the speaker into that bodily felt place. The speaking, coming through the body from the ground of world and Earth's gesturing, issues into speech that overflows the literal words.

Receiving the sense of the inner being of the speaker within our own inner being, vibrates through the felt sense of body; we wait in patience. We withhold quick responding, allowing what is heard and felt to resonate within bodily being. Communing with the other person in the field between us, leaving the presence of certainty, a response silently but tangibly gathers within.

An inward-turning point occurs point when the inner listening response of being in union with one speaking begins to transform into a verbal response. If the turning point is minimalized, not felt, then deep listening risks turning into shallow responding. The physical time interval of the turning point is less important than the soul-time that expands during this turning moment. The turning point has an expansive feeling when listening within and to the "between," not just to what the other person is saying. Speaking slows down as it gathers from the between rather than just shooting back pre-known concepts or using listening techniques, such as, "Yes, I understand," or "Oh, that's interesting." In the gathering, it is the un-said, the un-spoken that is being heard. Interpretation usually tries to enter. If one tries to directly speak the unsaid to the speaker, it will be felt as interpretation, or as an authority speaking, or a kind of pronouncement. So, the art of listening lies in this turning point.

The language of the turn-around speaks falteringly, full of pauses, shorter, sentences not quite worked out, pregnant disconnections occurring. The feeling of imperfection, the coming-to-birth of a response must be gently held or else slipping back into pre-formed concepts and words that lose the pauses and turn too quickly into pronouncement, and information occurs. The success of this kind of listening-responding, in terms of ordinary conversation, feels like a failure. Such an immediate feeling dissipates as the conversing lingers, ripens, and gradually opens new awareness rather than the seeming satisfaction of immediate knowing.

IX. The Oscillatory Motion between Self and Other

Rudolf Steiner, the founder of Spiritual Science and Anthroposophy, had a great insight concerning speaking with someone. While one person is speaking, the other person is "asleep." And then, when the person who was 'asleep' begins to speak, the first person sleeps. This, he says, is the way that ordinary conversation takes place. We put the other person asleep when we speak. That is, in usual conversation, listening goes unconscious because we are only hearing what we are going to say to the other person rather than what is being said, deeply.

Developing capacities of listening begins to open up that region of sleep alternating with wakefulness into an alert and open space between speaker and listener. Being within the Silence replaces sleepiness. The felt spaciousness between speaker and listener becomes the interior space of waking-silence, hearing what is being said while resting deeply in eternal Silence, simultaneously. Being fully awake while being asleep is the actual definition of contemplation.

As consciousness broadens and deepens, the gap between waking and sleep closes because sleep is not unconsciousness. It is the mode of consciousness within the depths of bodily being and also Earth-consciousness. Stones and minerals are conscious, and in the deepest of Silence, what they speak can be heard. The original people of the Americas say that a stone takes one breath a day.

In a conversation, the last thing said to the other person is the same as the last thought before going to sleep. Notice such a last thought; it does not suddenly disappear into sleep. It is as if the thought "melts" into fluid consciousness, goes from content to current, the same thing that occurs in deep meditation. This fluidity dissolving fixed content also happens when we speak and then stop and listen.

Sometimes, right when something is said, it is forgotten, before the next sentence is spoken. Then, when speaking again happens, it is like the first thought when waking up. The last thought before sleep reverberates into the depths of the body and into Earth. The first thought in the morning is Earth's response to that last thought. Human and Earth are held together as creating the Whole through this metaphysical/physical action of conversing. The little conversations of the day repeat this metaphysical/physical happening and resound like a mantra.

With this description, we have a way of working with listening as the contemplative path of being engaged with Earth's ongoing self-creation. Two or more people, together, become initiated into the Spiritual Earth through bodily presence.

Initiation typically occurs through individual meditative practice, alone, and the spiritual world is taken to be something other than the Earth, as Earth is taken literally and considered to be without spiritual value. From the usual spiritual point of view, Earth is taken as the place to get out of, the place of suffering and forgetfulness of the spiritual worlds, to be fought against, to eventually leave in death to then find where we really belong.

Spiritual-Earth, however, exists within the subtle spirit matrix, filled with spirits, the spirits of everything connected, self-creating matter as the expressive fullness of the Divine. The original people of this land knew Earth in this way—everything material as everything spirit. The spirits of the directions, the spirits of the animals, the spirits of the weather, everything material also as spirit.

Attuning to the process of conversation between two people is the prototypical template where this comprehensive spirit matrix begins to be noticed. Only now that the Earth we know is severely endangered does presence of the Spiritual-Earth, prototypal Earth in Her start becoming available to awakened bodily awareness. A different form of contemplation, contemplative co-creation with Earth, will now unfold through the next centuries.

X. Distinguishing Contemplative Listening from Psychological Listening

A psychologically oriented civilization imagines listening as integral to coming to some kind of psychological insight. People go to therapists to be listened to, to be heard, to be understood, to find themselves.

In developing the path of listening, I carefully stayed clear of using listening for psychological purposes. There is a great deal of interest in what happens between a patient and a therapist. The speaking-listening interactions of psychotherapy are understood as a psychic process of transference and countertransference, a different kind of "between" realm than developed here.

This theory of listening says that what goes on between therapist and patient, the "between" consists of projections by the patient of their felt sense of someone else than the person sitting across from them, such as father or mother, onto the therapist. Freud also discovered that similar counter-projections occur on the part of the therapist. In this model, two people relate through a third, the third of projection. In Jung's psychology, this model has become more sophisticated and approaches what we have been working with, but does not get here. He opens to archetypal figures that pattern relating and ultimately to more complex forms of individual relating. Earth is not even considered though magical transformations and synchronicities are recognized and have become the new concepts of depth psychology.

In depth psychology, the "between" of listening is called the "interactive field." Transference, as well as the interactive field is understood as the field of the archetypal figure of Eros in the archetypal psychology of James Hillman. In other forms of depth psychology, the field, or the third, can be any archetypal figure.

Those individuals who act out the archetypal figures of the interactive field carry the psychological label of "borderline personality." Such individuals lack the capacity to clearly differentiate their own being from that of the "between" but often develop psychic capacities, such as presence with the dead or certain kinds of clairvoyance. Some depth psychologists see the development of such capacities, beyond the difficulties of fusing with others, as the future of humanity. A more sophisticated version of the current emphasis on the "me-me" now become the "us-us" because psychology cannot get out of its excessive human-centeredness.

When one reads about what happens psychologically between people and sinks into the depth-psychological river, listening will probably frighten you. You may feel that you have to undergo deep psychological training in order not to get caught in the psychological pitfalls of listening. One does not want to fall in love with everyone listened to. And you don't want to be responsible for the confusion of boundaries between yourself and another person. And you don't want to be listening to someone who is "psychologically unstable" as you may be taken into the craziness. And, gosh, you want to avoid the currently popular psychological category of codependency.

Listening as unfolded in this writing is not psychologically tinged. It is a non-dual, contemplative, spiritual, bodily unfolding of a primary act of re-creation of human beings and simultaneously, of Earth. It has to be freely entered as a spiritual path—but one occurring within daily living rather than held as happening only through private meditative practice. Such a path emerges in this time because natural listening has disappeared and now has to become a conscious work.

One of the capacities needed on this path is that of distinguishing contemplative listening from paying psychological attention to "what is going on with the other person" or psychological attention to the interactive field between ourselves and another person. A further capacity concerns what is entailed in distinguishing spiritual-Earth listening from imposing spiritual pre-conceptions onto listening that utilize spiritual rather than psychological interpretations.

In a psychological approach to listening, whether occurring therapeutically or in daily life, what is heard is absence, void, and thus longing, need, desire, want, seeking comfort or to be comforted. In a contemplative approach to listening, what is heard is *fullness*. Nothing is lacking or absent. Everything is already here and present and the work is completely oriented toward developing the inner capacity of hearing the fullness of what is present, the Divine fullness of being human, and the Divine fullness of Earth's self-creating – as one.

Contemplative listening occurs within a cosmological context, within a felt sense of the Whole. If contemplative listening is taken as a set of techniques, it narrows into manipulative psychological listening.

The way through psychological listing into contemplative listening is simple. A conscious decision to enter contemplative listening is required. Like all contemplation, noticing and peeling away self-seeking belongs inherently to the path. Unlike other forms of contemplation, however, a very different sense of the Divine characterizes contemplative listening. Matter and spirit are experienced as entwined – through full bodily presence as both the instrument and medium of contemplation, which itself transforms in coming to subtle spiritual-sensory presence with Earth as expressing Divine presence.

The word 'decision' carries mental connotations, as if one decides after carefully considering various possibilities. If someone reads this writing and feels it is necessary to consider all that is written here and then decide – or not – to enter this path of contemplation, it can never happen. In reading this text, the mind has had to follow what is being said, *secondarily*. What is said here is first and primarily felt bodily. The mind alone would never decide to enter this path for—as a collective phenomenon, mind has already decided; collectively, we have embarked on the way of mentalism. The prevailing collective emotionalism is resistance to this path.

Noticing listening in these new ways requires the body to sink into its fullness. Changes are felt immediately. Body-oriented contemplative attention follows as long as mind is servant rather than leader. Attention now becomes more subtle and able; for example, to notice the relation between dreams and waking life. In the past, dreams seemed autonomous from the waking world and required symbolic interpretation to make connection with waking life. Now, the connections begin to be felt immediately upon waking.

Dream

I am outside, walking. The dirt is dry clay, the place clear, no sense of anything besides the earth. No trees, animals, plants, or birds. My right foot melts and becomes part of the earth. The absorption is extremely painful. I look down. I'm not frightened but lift up my foot and with a knife, try to cut away the earth that my foot melts into.

In this dream, the ego tries to prevent what is happening and attempts to restore the separation of earth from body. No interpretation is involved. The images are felt bodily and issue into speaking when awake.

Other dreams don't make this kind of immediate sense. Working with them, however, does not involve interpretation. They are written down, read contemplatively, and listened to in the manner described previously in relation to listening to other people. An inner assurance that dreams now belong to the contemplative listening process can be felt. There is no longer puzzlement over dreams. Dreams now indicate a peeling away of the civilizational filters of consciousness that now dominate.

For many centuries, Earth existence has undergone repression. Now, Earth is coming forward and cannot be constrained by abstract consciousness that separates the human being from Earth. Old, interpretive, and archetypal ways of "interpreting" dreams lose their power when contemplative listening begins. Contemplative listening transforms all dimensions of life and is not reserved only for engagement between ourselves and other people.

Does a person we engage in a contemplative way have to know what is happening? No. The Spirit awaits this possibility but has no agenda to make it happen because spirit lives free of linear time. If one individual engages in contemplative listening with another person, the world undergoes change.

If one person engages contemplatively with another person in conversation, a person who remains unaware might experience disappointment in the conversation because their egotism is bypassed, and the contemplative listener does not fall into it But what happened in the conversation will begin doing its transformative, receptive, creative work for both, for the world, and for Earth.

I am very grateful to Scott Scribner and Eric Hanson
for their fine editing work.

They turned confusion into a readable work.